IN THE HIGHEST

A 4-WEEK JOURNEY
to the Cross & the Risen King

C O U R T N E Y   J O S E P H   F A L L I C K

Hosanna in the Highest: A 4-Week Journey to the Cross & the Risen King
by Courtney Joseph Fallick

More Bible Studies

from Courtney & WomenLivingWell.org

Ecclesiastes: Wisdom for Living Well
6 Week In-Depth Study

Ruth: God's Amazing Love for You
5 Week In-Depth Study

Life Rhythms That Bring Rest
A 4-Week Guide to Making Your Home a Haven

Making Your Home a Haven
4-Week Bible Study

Rest and Release
4-Week Bible Study

Slowing Down for Spiritual Growth
4-Week Bible Study

Delight in the Lord
4-Week Bible Study

Don't Let Go! Holding Onto God When You Feel Like Giving Up, 31-Day Prayer Journal

Resting in His Presence
4-Week Bible Study on the Names of Jesus

Peace, Be Still
31-Day Christmas Prayer Journal

Books of the Bible

4-Week Study Journals

Numbers	1 Kings	Job	Mark	Galatians
Deuteronomy	2 Kings	Psalms	Luke	Ephesians
Joshua	1 Chronicles	Proverbs	John	Philippians
Judges	2 Chronicles	Ecclesiastes	Acts	Colossians
Ruth	Ezra	Isaiah	Romans	James
1 Samuel	Nehemiah	Jeremiah	1 Corinthians	
2 Samuel		Hosea	2 Corinthians	

and more to come...

Join the Good Morning Girls Community

Use hashtag #WomenLivingWell & share your daily SOAK on...

 Facebook.com/**GoodMorningGirlsWLW**

 Instagram.com/**WomenLivingWell**

Table of Contents

Introduction

And the crowds that went before Him and that followed Him
were shouting, "Hosanna to the Son of David!
Blessed is He who comes in the name of the Lord!
Hosanna in the highest!"

MATTHEW 21:9

Welcome to this 4-Week Journey to the Cross & the Risen King! As we walk through the life of Jesus—from His birth to His resurrection—I pray that this journal becomes a sacred space where you can meet with the Lord, reflect on His incredible love, and grow in your faith.

This journal is designed to guide you through a meaningful journey of reflection and worship. Each day includes:

- a carefully selected Bible passage to read
- a devotional to help you understand the key message of the scripture
- a reflection question to encourage deeper thought about how the passage applies to your life
- space to write your response
- space to journal your prayers, allowing you to pour out your heart to God and draw closer to Him

Each day's reading and journal prompts are intentionally designed to take just 10-15 minutes. As you commit to this journey, may you experience the love, hope, and joy of walking closely with Jesus, from the manger to the cross to the empty tomb. Let's begin…

On Palm Sunday, as Jesus rode into Jerusalem on a donkey, the crowd shouted "Hosanna in the Highest!" The word hosanna means *"save us"*. It is a cry for help. Yet, the same crowds that were full of hope and crying out to Jesus on that day, would shout *"crucify Him"* only five days later.

What the crowd did not realize is that the very thing they were crying out for, He would do! Jesus came to *"save us"*. He laid down his life for our sins and the story does not end there! Jesus rose from the dead proving that indeed He is the Son of God!

He is the King of Kings and the Lord of Lords! I am so excited to take this journey with you!

Let's Walk with the King!

Courtney
WomenLivingWell.org, GoodMorningGirls.org

The Birth of Jesus Christ
MATTHEW 1:18-25

18 Now the birth of Jesus Christ took place in this way. When his mother Mary had been betrothed to Joseph, before they came together she was found to be with child from the Holy Spirit. **19** And her husband Joseph, being a just man and unwilling to put her to shame, resolved to divorce her quietly.

20 But as he considered these things, behold, an angel of the Lord appeared to him in a dream, saying, *"Joseph, son of David, do not fear to take Mary as your wife, for that which is conceived in her is from the Holy Spirit.* **21** *She will bear a son, and you shall call his name Jesus, for He will save his people from their sins."*

22 All this took place to fulfill what the Lord had spoken by the prophet:

23 *"Behold, the virgin shall conceive and bear a son,*
    and they shall call his name Immanuel"
    (which means, God with us).

24 When Joseph woke from sleep, he did as the angel of the Lord commanded him: he took his wife, **25** but knew her not until she had given birth to a son. And he called his name Jesus.

WEEK 1

Jesus' Ministry

THE BAPTISM OF JESUS

And when Jesus was baptized, immediately He went up from the water, and behold, the heavens were opened to Him, and He saw the Spirit of God descending like a dove and coming to rest on Him; and behold, a voice from heaven said,

"This is my beloved Son,
with whom I am well pleased."

MATTHEW 3:16-17

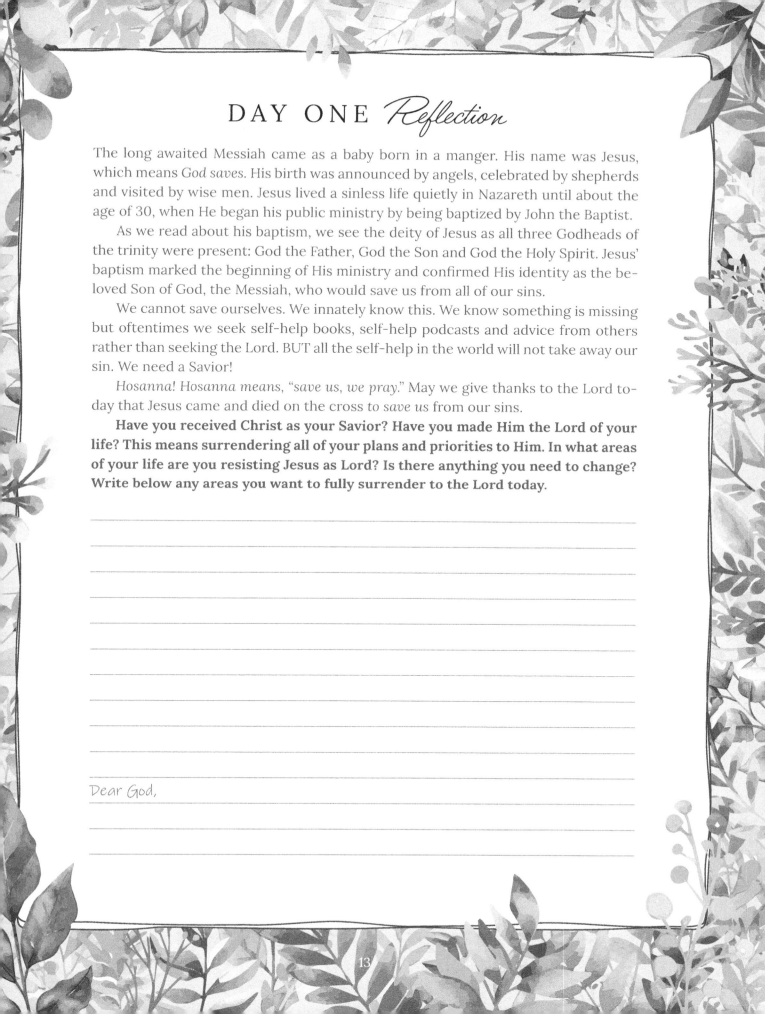

DAY ONE *Reflection*

The long awaited Messiah came as a baby born in a manger. His name was Jesus, which means *God saves*. His birth was announced by angels, celebrated by shepherds and visited by wise men. Jesus lived a sinless life quietly in Nazareth until about the age of 30, when He began his public ministry by being baptized by John the Baptist.

As we read about his baptism, we see the deity of Jesus as all three Godheads of the trinity were present: God the Father, God the Son and God the Holy Spirit. Jesus' baptism marked the beginning of His ministry and confirmed His identity as the beloved Son of God, the Messiah, who would save us from all of our sins.

We cannot save ourselves. We innately know this. We know something is missing but oftentimes we seek self-help books, self-help podcasts and advice from others rather than seeking the Lord. BUT all the self-help in the world will not take away our sin. We need a Savior!

Hosanna! Hosanna means, "save us, we pray." May we give thanks to the Lord today that Jesus came and died on the cross *to save us* from our sins.

Have you received Christ as your Savior? Have you made Him the Lord of your life? This means surrendering all of your plans and priorities to Him. In what areas of your life are you resisting Jesus as Lord? Is there anything you need to change? Write below any areas you want to fully surrender to the Lord today.

_____

_____

_____

_____

_____

_____

_____

_____

Dear God,

_____

_____

GREAT CROWDS FOLLOW JESUS

Jesus went throughout all Galilee, teaching in their synagogues and proclaiming the gospel of the kingdom and healing every disease and every affliction among the people. So his fame spread... and great crowds followed Him.

MATTHEW 4:23-25

DAY TWO *Reflection*

Jesus traveled and preached the gospel to all who would hear, and He healed many who were sick. This resulted in great crowds following Him. Not everyone who followed Him were sick physically but all of them were sick spiritually. The greatest sickness we have is the sickness of our sin. Sin damages our soul and separates us from God.

What's important to note is where Jesus preached the good news. He preached the good news in the Synagogues, where religious people attended. It is very easy to think that being born into a church family means that we're saved, but even good people need salvation from their sin.

Something I have always said to my children is that I don't want them to be good, I want them to be godly. There is a difference! While someone who is godly may also be good, someone who is good may not necessarily be godly. Being "good" refers to someone who does good deeds or who follows the rules. But being "godly" means you have a personal relationship with God and desire to obey and honor Him with your life which results in righteous living.

Are you leading a good life or a godly life? In what ways? Perhaps you've received Christ as your Savior long ago, but it's always good to remember that day. Write your salvation story below and think about how you have grown in godliness since then.

_____

_____

_____

_____

_____

_____

_____

Dear God,

_____

_____

SEEK FIRST HIS KINGDOM

But seek first the kingdom of God and his righteousness, and all these things will be added to you. Therefore, do not be anxious about tomorrow, for tomorrow will be anxious for itself. Sufficient for the day is its own trouble.

MATTHEW 6:33-34

DAY THREE *Reflection*

Jesus told his disciples to seek first the kingdom of God. Then He invited them to let go of all of their worries and anxieties and trust in Him. You see, when we seek God's kingdom first, God meets needs we didn't even know we needed both physically and spiritually.

Some people try to use material things to save themselves from their fear and anxiety, thinking that money and possessions will give them security and stability. For a moment, it may work but in time, those things only bring us more anxiety as we try to keep up on the hamster wheel of life. Our things were never meant to be what sustains us! Only God can fulfil our deepest longings.

Is there something heavy on your heart today? Jesus wants us to lay all of our worries and fears at the feet of Jesus. Every time we feel overwhelmed, we can echo the cry of *Hosanna*, remembering that our Savior has come to give us peace. Seeking Him first is not just a command—it's an invitation to experience the freedom and peace that only He can provide.

What are you worried about today? Is there something you are worried about in tomorrow? Seek God right now by writing out your concerns for today and to-morrow below and giving them all to Jesus.

_____

_____

_____

_____

_____

_____

_____

_____

_____

_____

_____

Dear God,

_____

_____

THE GOLDEN RULE

*So in everything, do to others
what you would have them do to you,
for this sums up the Law and the Prophets.*

MATTHEW 7:12 NIV

DAY FOUR *Reflection*

Today's reading is called the "Golden Rule", which says, "do to others as you would have them do to you." We tend to think that our hearts are good, but Jesus knows our hearts. He knows that we naturally act in our own self-interest rather than in the interest of others. And so, He gives us the bar with which to measure our selfish hearts.

Do you want someone to steal from you? Then don't steal from others.

Do you want someone to lie to you? Then don't lie to others.

Do you want someone to talk badly about you? Then don't talk badly about others.

Do you want someone to help you? Then help others.

Though the term "Golden Rule" is not used in scripture, Jesus says that summed up in this one command is all of the Prophets and Law. It is an extraordinary command! It is a command to love as Christ has loved us.

The bottom line is this: Treat others the way you want to be treated.

Take a moment right now and reflect on this command. How have you been treating others lately—those inside your home, those outside your home and those in your family? What changes do you need to make in your life to be more selfless and loving?

Dear God,

REST FOR YOUR SOUL

"Come to me,
all you who are weary and burdened,
and I will give you rest.
Take my yoke upon you and learn from me,
for I am gentle and humble in heart,
and you will find rest for your souls."

MATTHEW 11:28-29 NIV

DAY FIVE *Reflection*

Are you weary? Do you need rest? Not just physically but spiritually and emotionally, how are you doing? Jesus invites us to come to Him. All of us have burdens. Like a hiker weighed down with her backpack—we each have our own backpack, filled with stuff that weighs us down. We must remember that Jesus wants to carry our back-pack for us!

There are many things we try to turn to as an escape when we feel tired, but these escapes are only temporary fixes and often lead to even greater problems. Jesus calls us to turn to HIM, because He is the only one who can *save us* from our weary and burdened souls. He gives us true rest!

If you have ever flown on an airplane, then you know that when you fly you get a choice to either check your baggage or carry it on. I hope today you will choose to check all of your baggage and burdens with Jesus! Give it all to Him—don't carry it any longer.

What is weighing you down? What or whom do you turn to lately when you feel weary and burdened? Can you see how the rest you receive is only temporary? Share below how your escapes differ from running to Christ, and then write a prayer to God giving Him your burdens.

_____

_____

_____

_____

_____

_____

_____

_____

_____

_____

Dear God,

_____

_____

_____

TAKE UP YOUR CROSS

Then Jesus told his disciples,
"If anyone would come after me,
let Him deny Himself
and take up his cross and follow me.
For whoever would save his life will lose it,
but whoever loses his life for my sake will find it.

MATTHEW 16:24-25

DAY SIX *Reflection*

Jesus told his disciples, if they were going to follow Him, they were going to have to deny themselves and take up their cross to follow Him. This was not an easy saying for them to receive because they knew exactly what He meant. The cross was a picture of death.

Jesus invites us as well, to come and die to ourselves. BUT how do we walk this out in real life?

A lot of people say they want to follow Jesus, but they do not want to give up control of their lives. The life of a Christian—is a life of self-denial, surrender, sacrifice and of dying to the wants and desires of our flesh.

Jesus said that those who want to have life, must be willing to lose their lives to Him. He is the highest authority in our lives. He has the final word. If we want to keep control and the final word over our lives, we will one day stand before Him and discover that the life we thought we had, wasn't really life at all.

In what ways do you struggle to follow Jesus? Is there anything in your life you need to deny to follow Him more fully?

_____

_____

_____

_____

_____

_____

_____

_____

_____

_____

_____

Dear God,

_____

_____

DEATH AND RESURRECTION FORETOLD

As they were gathering in Galilee, Jesus said to them, "The Son of Man is about to be delivered into the hands of men, and they will kill Him, and He will be raised on the third day." And they were greatly distressed.

Matthew 17:22-23

DAY SEVEN *Reflection*

We can feel the tension rising as Jesus foretells his disciples of his coming death. The disciples were troubled when He said that He would be killed because while they looked to Him as their salvation, they completely misunderstood what kind of salvation He was offering. They thought He would save them from the oppression of the Roman Empire. They didn't realize that He had come to save them from a much greater oppression: sin and death.

But as the shadow of the cross loomed over Jesus' ministry, He continued to walk toward it willingly. Why? Because He knew that death would not be the final word! His disciples focused on the part where He said He would be killed and missed the hope of his resurrection!

Jesus came to fulfill the cry of Hosanna, "*save us*"! He knew that the pain of the cross was temporary and necessary for our salvation and the hope of the resurrection is eternal.

Do you find yourself misunderstanding what Jesus is doing in your life? Has He answered a prayer for you lately in a different way than you wanted? Has this caused you to be troubled? Take sometime today and ask the Lord to help you see what He is doing in your life right now.

_____

_____

_____

_____

_____

_____

_____

_____

_____

Dear God,

_____

_____

The Triumphal Entry
MATTHEW 21:1-11

¹ Now when they drew near to Jerusalem and came to Bethphage, to the Mount of Olives, then Jesus sent two disciples, ² saying to them, "Go into the village in front of you, and immediately you will find a donkey tied, and a colt with her. Untie them and bring them to me. ³ If anyone says anything to you, you shall say, 'The Lord needs them,' and He will send them at once."

⁴ This took place to fulfill what was spoken by the prophet, saying, ⁵ "Say to the daughter of Zion, 'Behold, your king is coming to you, humble, and mounted on a donkey, on a colt, the foal of a beast of burden.'" ⁶ The disciples went and did as Jesus had directed them. ⁷ They brought the donkey and the colt and put on them their cloaks, and He sat on them.

⁸ Most of the crowd spread their cloaks on the road, and others cut branches from the trees and spread them on the road. ⁹ And the crowds that went before Him and that followed Him were shouting,

> "Hosanna to the Son of David!
> Blessed is He who comes in the name of the Lord!
> Hosanna in the highest!"

¹⁰ And when He entered Jerusalem, the whole city was stirred up, saying, "Who is this?" ¹¹ And the crowds said, "This is the prophet Jesus, from Nazareth of Galilee."

WEEK 2

The Road to the Cross

HOSANNA!

Most of the crowd spread their cloaks on the road,
and others cut branches from the trees
and spread them on the road.
And the crowds that went before Him
and that followed Him were shouting,
"Hosanna to the Son of David!
Blessed is He who comes in the name of the Lord!
Hosanna in the highest!"

MATTHEW 21:8-9

DAY ONE *Reflection*

This portion of scripture is often called the Triumphal Entry of Jesus, and it fulfills the prophecy of Zechariah 9:9. The people recognized Jesus as the promised Messiah, crying out "Hosanna!" Their hearts were full of hope but the same people who shouted Hosanna to Jesus on that day, would shout *"Crucify Him!"* only 5 days later.

Jesus had come to bring them salvation, but not in a way they expected. This glorious king riding on a donkey did not look very much like a victorious king as He stood before Pilate beaten and bloody. He looked defeated and helpless. How could such a man bring salvation?

How often do we do this in our own prayer life? When a problem arises, we cry out, "Save me, God!" Yet, when God answers those prayers in a way we don't expect we complain "Don't save me like that, God!"

Consider today, the crowd spread their cloaks on the road before Jesus as a sign of honor to Him as the King. What do you need to lay down in your life to fully welcome Jesus as your King? Perhaps it's your fears, doubts, or even your own plans. Write a list below and surrender it all to Him.

_____

_____

_____

_____

_____

_____

_____

_____

_____

_____

_____

Dear God,

_____

_____

JESUS CLEANSES THE TEMPLE

And Jesus entered the temple and drove out all who sold and bought in the temple, and He overturned the tables of the money-changers and the seats of those who sold pigeons. He said to them, "It is written, 'My house shall be called a house of prayer,' but you make it a den of robbers." And the blind and the lame came to Him in the temple, and He healed them. But when the chief priests and the scribes saw the wonderful things that He did, and the children crying out in the temple, "Hosanna to the Son of David!" they were indignant,

MATTHEW 21:12-15

DAY TWO *Reflection*

Immediately following the triumphal entry of Jesus, He went into the temple courts and began to cleanse it. The temple was meant to be a sacred place of worship and prayer, but it had become a marketplace.

The people were buying and selling animals in the outer courts of the temple for the purpose of temple sacrifices. They sold animals like sheep, doves, pigeons and cattle to those who were arriving to celebrate the Passover. Jesus saw the greed of the merchants and He called them a "den of robbers."

Jesus did not stop after clearing the temple, He then went on to heal the blind and heal the lame. The children who saw this were amazed and cried out in praise "Hosanna!". But we see trouble looming in the distance, as the chief priests and scribes watched it all and were not pleased.

This passage is such a powerful picture of who Jesus is. He came to cleanse, restore and invite us into true worship.

Has the love of money tempted you away from the Lord in anyway? Is there anything in your life that's crowding out space for prayer and communion with God? Ask Jesus to cleanse your heart so you can worship Him more fully.

_____

_____

_____

_____

_____

_____

_____

_____

_____

_____

Dear God,

_____

_____

THE TWO GREATEST COMMANDMENTS

"You shall love the Lord your God with all your heart and with all your soul and with all your mind. This is the great and first commandment. And a second is like it: You shall love your neighbor as yourself. On these two commandments depend all the Law and the Prophets."

MATTHEW 22:37-39

DAY THREE *Reflection*

Jesus' death on the cross was a display of his unfailing love for us. He submitted to the Father's will even when it meant suffering unto death, and He loved us so much that He willingly gave his life to save us from our sins. When we reflect on the cross, we see that both greatest commandments were perfectly fulfilled in Jesus and because of His great love for us, we ought to love him with all of our heart, soul and mind and love others as well.

It's interesting to note that his command to love others is based on our natural love of self.

I know that there is a lot of talk these days about self-esteem and teaching our kids how to love themselves, but at the end of the day—none of us must teach our children to be selfish. We don't have to teach them to have desires to be loved, fed, clothed, or happy.

We all have a natural drive to be happy and think of ourselves first. So, this is not a command to stop loving ourselves but rather to love your neighbor AS yourself. This means in the same way that you want to be fed or loved or comforted, seek to feed, love and comfort others.

Jesus' love for us was sacrificial and selfless. That is the type of love we are to give to others. In what ways do you love God with all your heart, soul, and mind? Is there an area where you need to improve in your love for Him? In what ways can you live out your love for the Lord by loving others this week?

_____

_____

_____

_____

_____

_____

_____

_____

_____

Dear God, _____

_____

_____

WARNING OF FALSE TEACHERS

And Jesus answered them, "See that no one leads you astray. For many will come in my name, saying, 'I am the Christ,' and they will lead many astray. And you will hear of wars and rumors of wars. See that you are not alarmed, for this must take place, but the end is not yet.

MATTHEW 24:4-6

DAY FOUR *Reflection*

Jesus told his disciples that before He comes again, tribulation will grow more severe and the love of many will grow cold. In the midst of this tribulation, people will be seeking for someone to come and save them. Many will fall into deception as false teachers lead them astray.

Jesus told them to be sure that no one leads them astray. He alone is the only way, truth, and life. No man comes to the Father except through Him. (John 14:6) In a world filled with competing voices, we must remain rooted in the Word of God so that we are not deceived.

Many times, without realizing it, we look to people and things to save us from our insecurity, loneliness, or sorrow. We want to be saved from our troubles and trials and so we run to people rather than Jesus. In what ways do you find yourself turning to activities or people to escape your pain rather than God and his word?

_____

_____

_____

_____

_____

_____

_____

_____

_____

_____

_____

_____

Dear God,

_____

_____

_____

HIS WORD IS ETERNAL

*Heaven and earth will pass away,
but my words will not pass away.*

MATTHEW 24:35

DAY FIVE *Reflection*

From Genesis to Revelation, we see God's redemptive plan unfolding. Jesus' fulfillment of prophecy proves that God's word is true and reliable. May we be comforted by the fact that in a world that is ever changing, God's word does not change. His words are eternal.

Everything we see with our eyes is temporary and will one day fade away, but God's word will remain forever! Nations will rise and fall, and seasons will change but God's word will remain. As we study Jesus' journey to the cross, we see so many prophecies fulfilled. It is amazing. Jesus Himself is the living Word, sent to fulfill the ultimate promise of salvation.

Knowing that God's word is certain gives us a firm foundation to build our lives upon. His word is truth, and it is an anchor in times of trouble and a light in the darkness when we can't see what's ahead.

What is one promise from God's Word that you need to hold onto today? How can you live with an eternal perspective today, knowing that our God will reign forever, and His words will outlast the troubles of this world?

_____

_____

_____

_____

_____

_____

_____

_____

_____

_____

_____

Dear God,

_____

_____

THE FINAL JUDGEMENT

"When the Son of Man comes in his glory, and all the angels with Him, then He will sit on his glorious throne. Before Him will be gathered all the nations, and He will separate people one from another as a shepherd separates the sheep from the goats. And He will place the sheep on his right, but the goats on the left.

MATTHEW 25:31-33

DAY SIX *Reflection*

As we celebrate Jesus' first coming, it is good to remember that his second coming is still ahead! And though He came humbly as a baby in the manger at his first coming, at his second coming He says He will return as the King of kings, surrounded by heavenly hosts, and all the nations will bow before Him.

Jesus is not only our Savior, but He is the Good Shepherd and He knows his sheep by name. He knows YOU by name. Isn't that exciting?! The resurrection assures us that the same Jesus who conquered the grave will return in power and glory, and He will return as the righteous Judge and separate the sheep from the goats.

As we wait for that day, we are called to live with eternity in mind, faithfully following Him. John 10:3-4 says that Jesus knows his sheep by name. How does remembering this truth encourage you to live differently today? Are there any areas in your life where you can grow in obedience to your Shepherd?

_____

_____

_____

_____

_____

_____

_____

_____

_____

_____

_____

_____

Dear God,

_____

_____

JESUS FORETELLS HIS DEATH

When Jesus had finished all these sayings, He said to his disciples, "You know that after two days the Passover is coming, and the Son of Man will be delivered up to be crucified."

MATTHEW 26:1-2

DAY SEVEN *Reflection*

The Passover was coming, and Jesus began to prepare his disciples for what they were about to experience. He did not speak in parables like he had in the past. Instead, He plainly told them that in two days He would die.

Jesus was fully aware of what awaited Him. He knew the betrayal, the suffering, and the weight of our sin that He would carry. Yet, He didn't avoid it. His willingness to lay down His life was part of God's plan from the beginning.

It's important to note that this was during the time of the Passover. The Passover was a special time when God's people celebrated the remembrance of their deliverance from death and the slavery in Egypt. They knew Jesus was Messiah and that He had come to save them, but their understanding was that He would rescue them from the power of the Roman Empire. But Jesus came to rescue them from another power—the power of sin.

How does reflecting on Jesus' plan and willingness to go to the cross make you feel? How does it impact your relationship with Him? Write a prayer of thanksgiving below.

_____

_____

_____

_____

_____

_____

_____

_____

_____

_____

Dear God, _____

_____

_____

The Final Days

MATTHEW 26:1-16

¹ When Jesus had finished all these sayings, He said to his disciples, ² *"You know that after two days the Passover is coming, and the Son of Man will be delivered up to be crucified."*

³ Then the chief priests and the elders of the people gathered in the palace of the high priest, whose name was Caiaphas, ⁴ and plotted together in order to arrest Jesus by stealth and kill Him. ⁵ But they said, *"Not during the feast, lest there be an uproar among the people."*

⁶ Now when Jesus was at Bethany in the house of Simon the leper, ⁷ a woman came up to Him with an alabaster flask of very expensive ointment, and she poured it on his head as He reclined at table. ⁸ And when the disciples saw it, they were indignant, saying, *"Why this waste?* ⁹ *For this could have been sold for a large sum and given to the poor."*

¹⁰ But Jesus, aware of this, said to them, *"Why do you trouble the woman? For she has done a beautiful thing to me.* ¹¹ *For you always have the poor with you, but you will not always have me.* ¹² *In pouring this ointment on my body, she has done it to prepare me for burial.* ¹³ *Truly, I say to you, wherever this gospel is proclaimed in the whole world, what she has done will also be told in memory of her."*

¹⁴ Then one of the twelve, whose name was Judas Iscariot, went to the chief priests ¹⁵ and said, *"What will you give me if I deliver Him over to you?"*

And they paid Him thirty pieces of silver. ¹⁶ And from that moment He sought an opportunity to betray Him.

The Plot to Kill Jesus

ONE OF YOU WILL BETRAY ME

And the disciples did as Jesus had directed them, and they prepared the Passover. When it was evening, He reclined at table with the twelve. And as they were eating, He said, "Truly, I say to you, one of you will betray me."

MATTHEW 26:19-21

DAY ONE *Reflection*

Jesus gathered with his disciples to celebrate the Passover. Most likely they had done this before, but this time was different. Jesus knew the events that were about to unfold and so right there He reveals the shocking truth, "one of you will betray me."

Imagine the tension in the room. How could this be? They had done so much life together. They had walked with Jesus, witnessed his miracles, listened to his teachings and eaten many meals together and yet now one of his closest friends was about to hand Him over to die!

How could Jesus share the Passover meal with Judas, knowing that in a matter of hours, He would betray Him and set in motion the events that would lead to his trial? Judas' betrayal would result in Jesus being flogged, mocked, and ultimately crucified; and yet He was able to recline at the table in peace with his betrayer.

Have you ever been betrayed by someone close to you? Perhaps your best friend or a close family member has deserted you. How does remembering the composure and grace that Jesus extended to Judas encourage you? In what way has Christ's salvation brought you peace, even in painful times?

_____

_____

_____

_____

_____

_____

_____

_____

_____

_____

_____

Dear God,

_____

_____

_____

THE LAST SUPPER

Now as they were eating, Jesus took bread, and after blessing it broke it and gave it to the disciples, and said, "Take, eat; this is my body."

MATTHEW 26:26

DAY TWO *Reflection*

The disciples must have eaten the Passover meal many times with their families, but this time was different. Eating it with Jesus gave it a whole new meaning. The Passover meal was a picture of God's redemption of his people. It's unlikely that the disciples understood the significance of Jesus leading the Passover meal that evening, but as He went through each part of the meal, He was sharing the salvation story.

As Jesus broke the bread and shared it with His disciples, He explained that it represented His body, soon to be broken on the cross for them. The breaking of bread points to Jesus' willingness to be broken for us. He gave thanks, not because the cross would be easy, but because He was committed to fulfilling the Father's redemptive plan.

Jesus allowed his body to be beaten and bruised so that we could be saved and cleansed of all of our sin. Sit in that truth for a moment and soak it in. How does this impact your life today? When was the last time you thanked God for his sacrifice for you? Take the time to write about the day you were saved and write a prayer of thanksgiving below.

_____

_____

_____

_____

_____

_____

_____

_____

_____

_____

Dear God,
_____

_____

_____

THE INSTITUTION OF
THE LORD'S SUPPER

And He took a cup, and when He had given thanks He gave it to them, saying, "Drink of it, all of you, for this is my blood of the covenant, which is poured out for many for the forgiveness of sins. I tell you I will not drink again of this fruit of the vine until that day when I drink it new with you in my Father's kingdom."

MATTHEW 26:27-28

DAY THREE *Reflection*

The Passover meal is a celebration of the miracle God performed for the Israelites in Egypt. When the death angel went through Egypt taking the life of the firstborn, it "passed over" and saved the lives of the Israelites who had painted their doorposts with the blood of a lamb.

There is life in the blood! And now Jesus, the Lamb of God, would shed his blood to save us from our sins. What a beautiful picture of love and sacrifice.

In the midst of our busy lives, we are tempted to forget. We forget about Jesus' body broken for us. We forget about Jesus' blood poured out that covers our sins. We forget how much we are loved, how much we are forgiven and how grateful we are to be.

The ordinance of communion, practiced by the church body in community, forces us to slow down, be still, reflect and together remember our gift of salvation. We are told in 1 Corinthians 11:26, "*For as often as you eat this bread and drink the cup, you proclaim the Lord's death until He comes.*" This is a rhythm instituted by Jesus for our sake because He knows how easily we forget. We are to remember his death until He comes!

As you consider the saving blood of Jesus Christ, is there a friend, family member, or neighbor that has not yet cried out to Jesus for salvation? Write their names below and seek ways to share the gospel with them this week

Dear God,

JESUS FORETELLS PETER'S DENIAL

Peter answered Him, "Though they all fall away because of you, I will never fall away." Jesus said to Him, "Truly, I tell you, this very night, before the rooster crows, you will deny me three times." Peter said to Him, " Even if I must die with you, I will not deny you!" And all the disciples said the same.

MATTHEW 26:3-35

DAY FOUR *Reflection*

After dinner, Jesus sang a hymn with his disciples and then headed out to the Mount of Olives. In this somber moment, Jesus warned them that they were about to fall away. Peter could not even imagine such a thing happening and so he quickly spoke up and said, "Not me! I never will!"

Oh, how I love the heart of Peter! He was a man who loved Jesus deeply, but he was also human. When times are easy—it's easy to love Jesus. But he did not realize how weak he truly was, and how hard times were about to become. Peter was about to deny Jesus three times before dawn and Jesus knew this and yet still loved Him.

Friends, how many times have we failed Jesus? God is never surprised by our failures. He knows our weaknesses and yet He still loves us. His grace is greater than our failures. God was not done with Peter here; He went on to be a great man of faith and a leader in the early church.

In what ways do you feel like you have failed God? Is there an area where you tend to think you are stronger than you are? Acknowledge your weaknesses below and trust that God is not done with your story. He wants to use you even in the midst of your weaknesses and failures.

Dear God,

JESUS PRAYS

Then He said to them, "My soul is very sorrowful, even to death; remain here, and watch with me." And going a little farther He fell on his face and prayed, saying, "My Father, if it be possible, let this cup pass from me; nevertheless, not as I will, but as you will." And He came to the disciples and found them sleeping. And He said to Peter, "So, could you not watch with me one hour? Watch and pray that you may not enter into temptation. The spirit indeed is willing, but the flesh is weak."

MATTHEW 26:38-41

DAY FIVE *Reflection*

Jesus was troubled not only because He knew the tremendous level of physical suffering He was about to endure, but also because of the weight of guilt and shame He was about to bear as He became the final sacrifice for our sin.

Can you imagine how heavy that must have felt? When we imagine the weight of the most horrible sin, and then combine that with all of the sin of human history, that is what Jesus took upon Himself. No wonder He was overwhelmed with sorrow to the point of death!

In his darkest moment, Jesus invited his closest friends to stay with Him and watch and pray. But they fell asleep. *"The Spirit is willing, but the flesh is weak."*

How often have you fallen asleep in prayer? Don't you find that your heart is so willing, but your flesh is just simply weak. Even the disciples struggled, while Jesus remained faithful.

Jesus' command to "watch and pray" is not just for his disciples. It is for us today as well. How is your prayer life? Are you remaining spiritually alert, or have you grown weary?

_____

_____

_____

_____

_____

_____

_____

_____

_____

_____

_____

Dear God,

_____

_____

_____

BETRAYAL WITH A KISS

And He came up to Jesus at once and said,
"Greetings, Rabbi!" And He kissed Him.
Jesus said to Him, "Friend, do what you
came to do." Then they came up and
laid hands on Jesus and seized Him.

MATTHEW 26:49-50

DAY SIX *Reflection*

Judas' betrayal must have devastated the other eleven disciples. I am sure they stood and watched in disbelief as Judas betrayed Jesus with such an intimate act as a kiss. Yet, even in the face of betrayal, Jesus responded calling Judas his "friend".

Jesus' response shows how deep his unfailing love and grace runs. He knew Judas would betray Him and yet He never stopped being his friend. This serves as a reminder to us that Jesus was human, and He too suffered heartbreak and rejection. If someone close to you has hurt you, you are not alone. God sees your pain and He knows your heartache.

Later in Matthew 27, we see that Judas regretted his betrayal saying, "I have sinned." Friends, we don't always know the heart of a betrayer and why they make the choices they make but we can rest in knowing that at times, they know what they have done is wrong. It was too late for Judas. What had been done was done.

Reflect on a time when you felt betrayed. How does Jesus' response challenge you to give that person more grace? How does remembering that Jesus was not immune to heartache help you in the midst of your own hurt?

_____

_____

_____

_____

_____

_____

_____

_____

_____

_____

_____

Dear God,

_____

_____

PROPHECY FULFILLED

Do you think that I cannot appeal to my Father, and He will at once send me more than twelve legions of angels? But how then should the Scriptures be fulfilled, that it must be so?"

MATTHEW 26:53-54

DAY SEVEN *Reflection*

Have you ever considered that Jesus chose his suffering? He could have chosen not to go through the beatings, humiliation, pain, and death; but He knew that there was no other way to save us. This was God's plan for salvation from the beginning. The Scriptures had to be fulfilled.

I love how Jesus reminds the disciples of his divine power. He said that with a single word, He could have summoned twelve legions of angels. One Roman legion during Jesus' time consisted of around 6,000 soldiers. So, twelve legions would be 72,000 angels! What an overwhelming force that would have been! And yet, He chose restraint and obedience to the Father. Why? To fulfill scriptures and fulfill God's greater plan of salvation.

Obedience to God is a choice. Like Jesus, it is a choice we must make ahead of time to obey God no matter how hard it may be or how much it costs us. Is there a difficult choice God is asking you to make? Have you been tempted to come up with another plan? How do you see that obeying God brings about his will in your life?

_____

_____

_____

_____

_____

_____

_____

_____

_____

_____

_____

_____

Dear God,

_____

_____

The Crucifixion of Jesus
MATTHEW 27:32-44

32 As they went out, they found a man of Cyrene, Simon by name. They compelled this man to carry his cross.

33 And when they came to a place called Golgotha (which means Place of a Skull), **34** they offered Him wine to drink, mixed with gall, but when He tasted it, He would not drink it.

35 And when they had crucified Him, they divided his garments among them by casting lots. **3**

6 Then they sat down and kept watch over Him there. **37** And over his head they put the charge against Him, which read, *"This is Jesus, the King of the Jews."*

38 Then two robbers were crucified with Him, one on the right and one on the left. **39** And those who passed by derided Him, wagging their heads **40** and saying, *"You who would destroy the temple and rebuild it in three days, save yourself! If you are the Son of God, come down from the cross."*

41 So also the chief priests, with the scribes and elders, mocked Him, saying, **42** *"He saved others; He cannot save Himself. He is the King of Israel; let Him come down now from the cross, and we will believe in Him. 43 He trusts in God; let God deliver Him now, if He desires Him. For He said, 'I am the Son of God.'"*

44 And the robbers who were crucified with Him also reviled Him in the same way.

The Death & Resurrection of Jesus

JESUS ON TRIAL

What is your judgment?" They answered, "He deserves death." Then they spit in his face and struck Him. And some slapped Him, saying, "Prophesy to us, you Christ! Who is it that struck you?"

MATTHEW 26:66-68

DAY ONE *Reflection*

These verses are so heart-breaking to read. They hit Jesus and spit on Him and declared him *"worthy of death."* The hate, anger and pride within these men is hard to wrap my mind around. But what's even harder for me to wrap my mind around is the fact that Jesus was both fully man and fully God. He had the power to stop it and yet he chose to remain silent and willingly endure the pain of these religious leaders mocking and striking him. Why? Because of his love for you and me.

I am reminded that we all have sin in our hearts and that we all are in need of a Savior, whether we recognize it or not. These men would eventually see the power of God when Jesus rose from the grave. But this was all a part of God's plan. He had to endure all of this and go to the cross, so that we could be reconciled to God.

These men were the religious rulers and still felt no shame in beating and mocking Jesus. Even as believers, there are times when our lives deny the power of God; sometimes through our lack of faith or out of a fear of standing up for our beliefs.

Has there been an opportunity recently when you should have stood up for Christ, but didn't. How do you feel your actions could have been a denial of Jesus in that moment?

Dear God,

JESUS HANDED OVER TO PILATE

*When morning came, all the chief priests
and the elders of the people took counsel against
Jesus to put Him to death. And they bound Him
and led Him away and delivered Him
over to Pilate the governor.*

MATTHEW 27:1-2

DAY TWO *Reflection*

It is important to recognize that it was the religious leaders of the day, not the Roman political leaders, who plotted and planned how to have Jesus executed. It was the very people who taught the Torah, who knew the Law and Prophets more perfectly than anyone else. What they could not see was that while they thought they were executing a heretic, they were actually fulfilling the very Law they knew so well!

There are people who may know the Bible well, can quote a lot of Bible verses and recite all the major Bible stories, and yet not know the Lord. They may practice church traditions and never miss a Sunday of church, but they are still far from the Lord. They may follow all the rules and look good on the outside, but they do not have a relationship with Jesus.

Being religious and having a genuine and personal relationship with Jesus are different. While going to church and studying God's word is important, it does not save you. Saving faith transforms your heart and brings you into a right relationship with God through the forgiveness of your sins.

Do you consider yourself religious? God wants us to know Him, not just about Him. How well do you know God? In what ways do you need to deepen your relationship with God?

_____

_____

_____

_____

_____

_____

_____

_____

_____

_____

Dear God,

_____

_____

JESUS IS SILENT

But when He was accused by the chief priests and elders, He gave no answer. Then Pilate said to Him, "Do you not hear how many things they testify against you?" But He gave Him no answer, not even to a single charge, so that the governor was greatly amazed.

MATTHEW 27:12-14

DAY THREE *Reflection*

Do you sometimes wonder what would've happened if Jesus had answered Pilate? He could have spoken up and given an answer that would have changed everything, right? But He didn't.

Most of us tend to speak up when we are wrongfully accused but Jesus knew what needed to happen. His silence was strength. He was trusting in the Lord's plan. He was fulfilling prophecy (Isaiah 53:7).

There are times when we may think that God is silent or that He is not working at all. But through Jesus' silence, God's plan of redemption was being fulfilled.

Has there been a time in your life, when you were crying out to God and He was silent? Did his silence cause you to think He wasn't working in your life? Looking back, how can you see that God was still working, even in his silence?

Dear God,

JESUS IS MOCKED

And they stripped Him and put a scarlet robe on Him, and twisting together a crown of thorns, they put it on his head and put a reed in his right hand. And kneeling before Him, they mocked Him, saying, "Hail, King of the Jews!" And they spit on Him and took the reed and struck Him on the head. And when they had mocked Him, they stripped Him of the robe and put his own clothes on Him and led Him away to crucify Him.

MATTHEW 27:28-31

DAY FOUR *Reflection*

Jesus' followers must have felt very confused as Jesus was led away to be executed. How could He be their Messiah—their sent one? How could He be their victorious king? Jesus, the Savior of the world, was beaten, bloody, and being led away to his execution like a common criminal. How could He save the world now? But what seemed hopeless to them was all part of God's plan for reconciliation with God.

The soldiers mocked Jesus. They mocked Him by draping a scarlet robe over his beaten body. They mocked Him by putting a crown of thorns onto his head. They mocked Him by putting a reed in his right hand like it was a scepter and then they mocked Him by pretending to worship Him saying "Hail! King of the Jews!" And if all of that was not terrible enough, then they spit on Him and struck Him.

Oh, what a price that was paid for our sins! Jesus remained silent. He could have stopped them, but He went all the way to the cross out of his love for you and me. What a deep deep love He has for us that He would lay down his life in such a sacrificial way.

How can you honor Jesus today as the King of your life? Spend time in prayer today thanking Him for enduring the pain of the cross for your salvation.

_____

_____

_____

_____

_____

_____

_____

_____

_____

_____

_____

Dear God,

_____

_____

THE DEATH OF JESUS

Now from the sixth hour there was darkness over all the land until the ninth hour. And about the ninth hour Jesus cried out with a loud voice, saying, "
Eli, Eli, lema sabachthani?" that is,
"My God, my God, why have you forsaken me?"

And some of the bystanders, hearing it, said, "
This man is calling Elijah."

And one of them at once ran and took a sponge,
filled it with sour wine, and put it on a reed
and gave it to Him to drink. But the others said,
"Wait, let us see whether Elijah will come to save
Him."

And Jesus cried out again with a loud voice
and yielded up his spirit.

And behold, the curtain of the temple was
torn in two, from top to bottom.

And the earth shook, and the rocks were split. The tombs also were opened. And many bodies of the saints who had fallen asleep were raised, and coming out of the tombs after his resurrection they went into the holy city and appeared to many.

When the centurion and those who were with Him, keeping watch over Jesus, saw the earthquake and what took place, they were filled with awe and said,

"Truly this was the Son of God!"

MATTHEW 27:45-54

DAY FIVE *Reflection*

Darkness covered the land. As Jesus bore the weight of our sin that separates us from God, He cried out, *"My God, my God, why have you forsaken me?"* Then He yielded up his spirit and died.

Just when it seemed that God was silent and all hope was lost, the first rumblings of God's eternal plan was heard as the curtain in the temple was miraculously torn from top to bottom, opening up the Holy of Holies for the very first time. Nature joined in as the earth shook and the rocks were split.

The Son of God did what no human could ever do! He paid for all our sin on the cross and conquered death, hell, and the grave. Even the Roman centurion recognized, *"Truly, this was the Son of God!"*

This moment in history changes everything!

Simply stand in awe of this gift today. We now have the hope of new life both here on earth and in heaven. How has Christ's sacrifice on the cross changed your life?

_____

_____

_____

_____

_____

_____

_____

_____

_____

_____

_____

_____

Dear God,

_____

_____

THE GUARD AT THE TOMB

The next day, that is, after the day of Preparation, the chief priests and the Pharisees gathered before Pilate and said, "Sir, we remember how that impostor said, while He was still alive, 'After three days I will rise.' Therefore order the tomb to be made secure until the third day, lest his disciples go and steal Him away and tell the people, 'He has risen from the dead,' and the last fraud will be worse than the first." Pilate said to them, "You have a guard of soldiers. Go, make it as secure as you can." So they went and made the tomb secure by sealing the stone and setting a guard.

MATTHEW 27:62-66

DAY SIX *Reflection*

The chief priests and Pharisees were scared. They remembered Jesus' claim to rise on the third day and so they went to great lengths to secure the tomb. They rolled a large stone in front the entrance, sealed it and then put soldiers beside the tomb to prevent anyone from entering. But no human effort—no matter how strong, could stop the resurrection of Jesus Christ!

Though the religious leaders called Jesus an imposter, their actions proved that deep down, they feared His words might be true. They tried to secure the tomb, but a sealed tomb and a guarded entrance could not keep Jesus in the grave! Nothing can stop God's plan from being fulfilled!

Our God is in control. Nothing man tries to do can stop Him. Even when things seem impossible, our God is greater. His promises are sure. We can fully trust in Him!

Are you facing an obstacle today that feels impossible? Is fear or doubt creeping in? How does remembering the power of our God grow your confidence in Him today?

_____

_____

_____

_____

_____

_____

_____

_____

_____

_____

_____

_____

Dear God,

_____

_____

HE IS RISEN!

Now after the Sabbath, toward the dawn of the first day of the week, Mary Magdalene and the other Mary went to see the tomb. And behold, there was a great earthquake, for an angel of the Lord descended from heaven and came and rolled back the stone and sat on it. His appearance was like lightning, and his clothing white as snow. And for fear of Him the guards trembled and became like dead men. But the angel said to the women, "Do not be afraid, for I know that you seek Jesus who was crucified. He is not here, for He has risen, as He said. Come, see the place where He lay."

MATTHEW 28:1-6

DAY SEVEN *Reflection*

He is risen! Those are the words that the women who went to the grave to mourn and tend to Jesus' body heard. As the earth shook, an angel appeared and rolled back the stone. The soldiers were suddenly gripped with fear, but the women were told to not be afraid, Jesus was alive! Don't miss the next phrase, *"just as He said."*

That's our God! He is faithful. What He says He will do—He will do.

From the humble manger in Bethlehem to the triumphant cries of "Hosanna" on Palm Sunday, to the cross and the empty grave, Jesus' journey was one of love, sacrifice, and redemption. Every step He took was intentional, fulfilling the promises of God and paving the way for our salvation. The cross, where He bore the weight of our sin, and the empty tomb, where death was forever defeated, testify to His unending power and grace.

As we reflect on Jesus' life, death, and resurrection, let us hold fast to the hope that Jesus brings—hope that transforms mourning into joy, fear into faith, and death into eternal life. Let us declare, with hearts full of gratitude and worship, *"Hosanna in the highest! Blessed is He who comes in the name of the Lord!"*

How does the life, death, and resurrection of Jesus inspire you to live each day with hope and purpose, proclaiming 'Hosanna in the highest' through your words and actions?

Dear God,

The Great Commision

MATTHEW 28:18-20

¹⁶ Now the eleven disciples went to Galilee, to the mountain to which Jesus had directed them. ¹⁷ And when they saw Him they worshiped Him, but some doubted.

¹⁸ And Jesus came and said to them, *"All authority in heaven and on earth has been given to me. ¹⁹ Go therefore and make disciples of all nations, baptizing them in the name of the Father and of the Son and of the Holy Spirit, ²⁰ teaching them to observe all that I have commanded you. And behold, I am with you always, to the end of the age."*

Jesus' Ascension

ACTS 1:6-11

[6] So when they had come together, they asked him, "Lord, will you at this time restore the kingdom to Israel?"

[7] He said to them, *"It is not for you to know times or seasons that the Father has fixed by his own authority.* [8] *But you will receive power when the Holy Spirit has come upon you, and you will be my witnesses in Jerusalem and in all Judea and Samaria, and to the end of the earth."*

[9] And when he had said these things, as they were looking on, he was lifted up, and a cloud took him out of their sight.

[10] And while they were gazing into heaven as he went, behold, two men stood by them in white robes, [11] and said,

"Men of Galilee, why do you stand looking into heaven? This Jesus, who was taken up from you into heaven, will come in the same way as you saw him go into heaven."

For Further Reading

STILL STANDING: HOW TO LIVE IN GOD'S LIGHT WHILE WRESTLING WITH THE DARK

by Courtney Joseph Fallick

How do you stand up after life knocks you down?

That's the question Courtney Joseph Fallick asked herself when she entered the darkest season of her life. She found herself drowning in fear, shame, and grief, while God seemed silent.

Opening up about her husband's deep betrayal and abandonment, Courtney shows you how to rise up after your own heart-crushing struggles, cling to God's promises, and move forward stronger than before.

Sharing the hard-fought lessons she learned, she helps you:

- hold on to your faith when life wounds you
- stand back up—and keep standing—after being knocked down
- overcome discouragement and disillusionment
- heal your hurts and let go
- recover from loss and grief
- find enough strength, joy, rest, and peace for each day

This dark valley *will* end. Here is the infusion of hope you need to rise, live well, and walk with the King.

Made in the USA
Monee, IL
19 February 2025